Sip & Savor

Drinks for Party and Porch

JAMES T. FARMER III

GIBBS SMITH

TO ENRICH AND INSPIRE HUMANKIND

*For my sisters, Maggie and Meredith,
and my favorite brother-in-law, Zach.
Sipping and savoring with y'all just
might be my favorite pastime.*

*Love,
Brubbs*

First Edition
12 14 16 15 13
1 3 5 4 2

Text © 2012 by James T. Farmer III
Photographs © 2012 by James T. Farmer III and Maggie Yelton except
pages 9 and 60 from Shutterstock

Published by
Gibbs Smith
P.O. Box 667
Layton, Utah 84041

1.800.835.4993 orders
www.gibbs-smith.com

Designed by Michelle Farinella Design

Printed and bound in China
Gibbs Smith books are printed on either recycled, 100% post-consumer waste,
FSC-certified papers or on paper produced from sustainable PEFC-certified
forest/controlled wood source. Learn more at www.pefc.org.

Library of Congress Cataloging-in-Publication Data

Farmer, James T.
Sip & savor : drinks for party and porch / James T. Farmer III. — 1st ed.
p. cm.
Includes index.
ISBN 978-1-4236-2484-4
1. Beverages. 2. Entertaining. 3. Cookbooks. I. Title. II. Title: Sip and savor.
TX815.F28 2012
641.2—dc23
2011043873

❧ *Contents* ❧

❋ *Introduction* ❋

Sip and savor: to enjoy a drink in a luxurious fashion and measure. These very words evoke a lifestyle full of afternoons lulling on porches, of watching sunsets over coastal marshes, of stopping to literally smell the roses and taking delightful enjoyment in a simple beverage: a beverage that perhaps takes you back through the channels of nostalgia to memorable moments of days gone by.

Maybe it is lemonade on grandmother's porch or a warm mug of cider during the holidays or even a glass of tea infused with garden goodness—food and good drinks in turn mark our memories with points of reference poised to remind us of happy times. We hold our glasses, mugs, cups, and even jars and toast to a life where sipping and savoring is de rigueur. These drinks are meant to remind us of the importance of appreciating and relishing the first berries of spring, the ripest of summer's best produce, the tastes and smells of autumn's palette, and the valuable warmth of a wintertime toast. With each season, new flavors and textures can spice our days.

Porches and parties boast as perfect locales and venues for sipping and savoring, and so many of these drinks are apropos for both! From the simplicity of swingin' or rockin' on the porch, to a brouhaha of fabulous brews, both porches and parties are my favorite spots to sip and savor. Teas and cafés; citrus blends and lemonades; nectars, fizzes and sparklers; cordials, punches and milky concoctions fill these pages and hopefully will grace your porch and party, as well as wet your whistle!

Upon arrival on a porch, to a party or in a home, for that matter, it is a refreshing beverage that is often first offered. We must rejuvenate our bodies and spirits with drink, not by gulping the liquids of life but savoring each drop with purpose and maybe even pizzazz! Water may be our lifeline, but fun drinks can be our lifestyle! Pour a glass of your favorite blend and toast to life, to blessings, and joy.

Now, with these recipes and inspirations for a bevy of beverages, sip and savor these drinks for days to come—days that I hope are filled truly with porches, parties, and all the celebrations life can afford.

Simple Syrups are Simply Fabulous!

From waking up a glass of tea with a punch of pizzazz to taming a tart lemon or interjecting the very essence of a season into your favorite drink, simple syrups are indispensable!

Just a 1:1 ratio of water and sugar, simple syrup in its very basic form livens any beverage with delightful sweetness. Simple syrup can be stored in the fridge indefinitely (but it won't last!). This accoutrement to the brews and blends that we sip and savor can be at hand all the time.

As the vehicle to sweetness for our favorite drinks, this is also the medium to interpose the seasons' best offerings. Mint, thyme, basil, ginger, rosemary, honey and host of other herbs and flavors all meld together to form sweetly infused syrups that awaken the floral, fruity and earthen notes in our favorite teas, punches and lemonades.

The base is the same and the results are too—grand and elegant—from the simplest of gestures, a truly simple syrup.

Basic Simple Syrup

1 cup sugar

1 cup water

Bring sugar and water to a boil and then turn down heat, stirring all the while. Once the sugar is dissolved, allow to cool. Store in an airtight container in the refrigerator indefinitely.

❋ Herbal Simple Syrup ❋

Be brazen and bold with your choices of herbs, such as chocolate or orange mint, lemon thyme, 'BBQ' rosemary, 'African Blue' basil, or lavender. These amazing varieties within a flavor family are terrific twists to everyday herbs!

Makes 1 1/2 cups

2–3 tablespoons freshly chopped herb of choice

1 cup sugar

1 cup water

Chop, mash, mince, or leave whole the leaves of your herb of choice.

Bring sugar and water to a boil then toss prepared herb into the water. Allow to boil for 1 minute. Reduce the heat and then simmer for 10 minutes, stirring frequently to dissolve the sugar. Strain the syrup and discard the herb leaves. Syrup can be stored in an airtight container and refrigerated indefinitely.

❋ Mint Simple Syrup ❋

Makes 1 1/2 cups

1 cup water

1 cup sugar

3–4 leafy stems of mint

Place the water and sugar in a saucepan over medium heat. Stir until the sugar dissolves then bring to a boil. Boil 3 minutes and then remove from the heat. Drop in the mint leaves and push them down into the syrup. Leave to cool. When cool, pour into an airtight jar and refrigerate.

Simple Syrups are Simply Fabulous!

❀ *Ginger Simple Syrup* ❀

Makes 1 1/2 cups

1 cup sugar

1 cup water

1/4 cup peeled and sliced
  fresh gingerroot

1 cup sugar

1 cup water

Bring sugar, water, and gingerroot to a boil. Allow to boil for 1 minute. Reduce the heat and then simmer for 10 minutes, stirring constantly to dissolve the sugar. Strain the syrup and discard the bits of ginger. Syrup can be stored in an airtight container and refrigerated indefinitely.

❀ *Lemon Thyme–Infused Brown Sugar Simple Syrup* ❀

Makes 1 1/2 cups

1 cup packed brown sugar

4 small stems of lemon thyme

1 cup water

Combine all ingredients in a small pot and warm thoroughly to dissolve the sugar and create a liquid. Allow to steep for 5 minutes, then strain the thyme leaves. Serve with your favorite drink and refrigerate the rest.

Simple Syrups are Simply Fabulous!

Teas & Cafés

HOW TO MAKE TEA

I'm known for my tea. My teenage sister and her friends call it "flower tea" or "fruit loop tea," and they're right! I use one bag of Earl Grey with four bags of "normal" tea. That one bag infuses this steeped staple of the South with a bouquet of floral and fruit essence. Teas, like wine and coffee, get their flavors from the regions where they are grown. Earl Grey is natural black tea with oil of bergamot, which is oil derived from the bergamot orange, thus the fruity/floral hint.

I love tea and everything associated with it, but my particular favorite accompaniment is sugar. I make a simple syrup for my iced tea and then mix the steeped tea with the syrup and some water. Tea should be steeped for 5–6 minutes max and then mixed with the sugar solution and served over ice.

Mint, limes, and lemons are great garnishes for adding more depth to the flavor. I prefer lime or sweet Meyer lemons. I also infuse the simple syrup with a few stalks of rosemary during the fall and winter months: The pine-like rosemary seems appropriate for the season. For a stronger flavor, you can add the rosemary to the boiling water and tea bags.

Following is my recipe for Farmer's Tea. I don't measure, thus the range in proportions.

Makes about 2 pitchers

8–10 cups water, divided

4 tea bags of your choice

1 tea bag Earl Grey

1 1/2 cups sugar

Lime wedge for garnish

Bring 6–7 cups of water to a rolling boil. Add 4 bags of Lipton (or whatever brand you prefer) and 1 bag of Earl Grey and remove from heat. Let the tea bags steep for about 5 minutes near the warm eye of the stove.

In a separate saucepan, add 1 1/2 cups of sugar to about 2–3 cups of water (I use a 1:2 ratio) over medium-low heat; stir until sugar is dissolved and the water becomes a somewhat clear syrup. If you let the sugar water continue to boil, you'll have the makings for candy and not tea!

Combine the steeped tea and simple syrup in a large pitcher, or split between two half-gallon pitchers. If you're using a glass pitcher, be sure to have a metal knife or spoon to pour the tea over so the hot liquid doesn't bust the glass.

Fill the pot with the tea bags in it one more time with water and add that water to the pitcher; you can add a bit more water to suite your taste. Stir with a long knife or spoon. Serve over ice and with wedges of lime. Remember, tea continues to steep or "get stronger" as it sits, so it's weakest when first made).

Summer Herb Peach Tea

I love tea. I love summertime. I love peaches. Mix them all together and I'm simply thrilled! This is an easy and elegant drink that looks great in crystal goblets or Mason jars, and it pairs well with many meals or can simply be served as a starter beverage. This drink is one that changes as summer progresses. My herb availability waxes and wanes and different peach varieties come into season. For a twist, you can use white peaches. Regardless, one thing does not change, and that is how divine this drink is!

Makes about 7 cups

3 bags chamomile tea

6 cups water

1 handful herb leaves (equal parts rosemary, basil, lemon thyme, mint, lavender or some of your favorites)

2 peaches cut into wedges; reserve some for garnish

Peach nectar, honey, or simple syrup, optional

Bring water to a boil and add the tea bags and herbs. Allow to steep for 5 minutes. Pour the tea and herbs through a fine mesh strainer into your serving or storage container. Add peach wedges and allow them to infuse the tea while it is warm.

If you care to sweeten, use peach nectar, honey, or simple syrup. This tea is naturally flavorful, so sweetening this concoction simply gilds the lily. Garnish with peach wedges and mint.

Teas & Cafés

Honeydew Green Tea ✾

"Honey, do you care for a drink?"

"Honey, I surely do!"

This will be the conversation between you and your honey, for the delicate flavors of honeydew melon and green tea meld together for a refreshment so visually enchanting that the taste is nothing short of magical. Combining elegant airs of fresh melon, crisp notes of tea, and a bit of herbal sensation sweetness, this beverage is a treat on the hottest of summer days and the perfect way to relax and unwind from the heat of the day. With its health benefits aside, green tea might also be a wonder drink for our waistlines! Serve some of the blended honeydew melon in the hollowed rind.

Gather some of your garden's freshest mint, thyme or basil for herbal flair, find a perfectly ripe honeydew melon, and then brew and blend a treat for you and your honey!

Serves 6–8

2 cups water

1 baker's dozen fresh herb leaves (mint, mild basil, thyme, or your choice)

4 bags green tea

1/3 cup Simple Syrup (Basic or Herbal; see pages 5 and 6) or honey

1 small to medium honeydew melon

1 1/2 cups ice cubes

Bring water to a boil. Add about a dozen or so mint leaves and tea bags to the boiling water. Allow to steep for 3–4 minutes then discard the tea bags and herb leaves. Sweeten the tea with simple syrup or honey. Chill tea before serving.

Scrape out the inside of the melon and add to a blender with the ice. Spoon the slushy melon puree into ice-cold green tea and garnish with herbs.

❋ *A James Farmer* ❋

I have to start my day with a glass of orange juice. Not just any, mind you, but good, pulpy orange juice that you have to chew. Take this morning starter and add it to my Farmer's Tea, and you have a James Farmer.

My Farmer's Tea is flavored with Earl Grey, which derives its unique taste from the oil of the bergamot orange, a close cousin to our typical juice oranges. With such a close family tie, the combo of Farmer's Tea with orange juice is perfectly apropos.

This drink is great year-round and can change with seasons by infusing seasonal herbs.

Makes however much you want

**Equal parts Farmer's Tea
    and orange juice**
Serve over ice
**Garnish with orange or
    favorite citrus wedges**

An Arnold Palmer

While on the subject of adding citrus to tea, the known classic is an Arnold Palmer. Mix together half tea and half lemonade and there you have it! This was supposedly the drink of choice for Mr. Palmer when he was through with the back nine or coming off the greens. You can use sweet or unsweetened tea, depending on your desire for sugar.

Serves 2

2/3 cup lemonade
2/3 cup tea
Pour over ice and enjoy

I love orange juice. I love sweet tea. Mix the two together and wowza! Here is the trick, though: you have to use good orange juice and good tea. If the foundation is not strong, then your drink will merely be a house of cards, destined to fall with the slightest stir.

Fresh-squeezed orange juice is a delicacy in and of itself. Though life doesn't allow me to prepare freshly squeezed orange juice every morning, I find solace in the fact that Simply Orange, Natalie's Orchid Island, and Whole Food's 365 brands are readily available. The ratio, a 1:1 makeup of tea to juice, is fundamental to enjoying this beverage. Add a splash of Russian drinking water (vodka), and this drink becomes an adult beverage in a splash—I mean flash!

An Arnold Palmer or a "James Farmer"—take your pick or take them both! I'm sure they will be a hit at your next dinner party, brunch or soiree. Hopefully, barkeeps around the Deep South will recognize a request for a "James Farmer," but if not, feel free to educate them! Ha! From this Farmer's bar to yours, salut!

Iced Pomegranate Oolong Tea

My mother's maiden name is Granade, and the pomegranate dons our family crest. Literally the "apple of Grenada," the pomegranate has fascinated, enchanted, nurtured, and delighted mankind for thousands of years. The pomegranate craze is abounding and I'm thankful, for the fruit is super high in benefits, tasty, and absolutely gorgeous just to gaze upon.

For Christmas one year, one of my dear clients gave me a box of Pomegranate Oolong Tea. The canister itself was lovely and the tea was lusciously divine, refreshing, palate-pleasing, and fantastic iced or warm. This tea garnered my approval, for the flavor was so crisp and clean that no sugar was really needed. Basically, brewing the tea and adding a few pomegranate arils is all it takes to enjoy this drink. A garnish of mint never hurts either.

Makes 2 cups or glasses

1 bag pomegranate oolong tea

2 cups water

Bring water to a boil and toss in the tea bag. Remove from heat and allow the tea to steep for 5 minutes. Serve over ice and garnish with pomegranate arils and mint.

❋ *Raspberry Mint Tea* ❋

The smoothness of raspberry puree mixed with Farmer's Tea and served over ice is truly delightful. A stunning color falling somewhere in the range of claret, ruby, and garnet, this drink is sure to be an all-star from your kitchen's lineup. Speaking of the gorgeous hues this drink takes on, a pinch of baking soda will help preserve the fresh raspberry color.

This is so easy and makes for an extremely elegant presentation. Whether or not you have a blender, the raspberries are so soft that they are easy to puree by hand. A blender does help mince and finely smooth out the berries and mint, but some elbow grease makes for just as lovely a result.

Serves 8 or more

1 pint fresh raspberries, a few reserved for garnish

3 sprigs mint, leaves removed and reserved

Pinch of baking soda

1/2 gallon (8 cups) Farmer's Tea, sweetened of course

Puree or mash by hand the raspberries, mint and soda. Add to the tea. Mix well and serve over ice. Garnish with raspberries and mint.

Note Mint syrup can be used to sweeten the tea to taste or to control the sweetness if using unsweetened tea. This concoction can also be frozen or blended with ice to make a slushy or a granita.

❋ *Mrs. Betty's Sun Tea* ❋

Sun tea has long been a tradition not only in the Deep South but anywhere a few hours of strong sunlight, some tea, and a vessel could collaborate and create this classic beverage.

In the South, we celebrate and mourn, birth and bury, and bless and curse with food. Whether you have tied the knot, passed from this life or given life to a newborn, food and drink can toast the occasion. Many denominations in the South are even tagged by their casserole dishes, buffet items, cocktails or lack thereof. Having grown up Baptist, we were the latter. So we celebrated with tea!

"One thing I will always remember about what nice food and things folks brought us when you were born," my mother reminisced, "is Mrs. Betty's Sun Tea." She was helping me make a batch of the relished drink. "It was so good: steeped just right, sweetened just right and perfect for the hot June day you came home." Being brought home to a house filled with Baptist food and sun tea set the tone for my life, I'm afraid. Good food and good tea are de rigueur! With the hot June sun pressing down on our small Georgia town, one of the best ways to beat the heat as to use it to make tea.

Makes a pitcher or so, about 8 cups

¹/₂ gallon (8 cups) water

5 tea bags of your choice

Basic Simple Syrup to taste (see page 5)

Herbs or fruit for garnish, optional

Pour the water into a glass container with a lid, and drop in the tea bags. Screw the lid on and allow the tea bags to steep in the glass container in the full sun for 3–5 hours, or until it reaches the desired strength. The hotter the sun shines, the faster the tea will be made.

Sweeten to taste and serve over ice. Garnish with summer herbs or fruit.

A FEW NOTES ON SUN TEA

One reason this tea has been quite popular in the summer months is not only for the strength of the sunshine, but it was one way to keep the kitchen temperature down during the heat of the day: one less burner to burn.

Always use a clean container with a tight-fitting lid. Large Mason or Ball jars, pitchers with lids, and other containers are all good candidates. Allowing the tea to steep in this slow manner brings out other essences not as easily detected when using boiling water. This method is simply elegant to bring out the tea's natural bouquet.

I prefer to mix up the regimen and throw in a bag or two of Earl Grey. Try it with different herbal or fruit-infused teas for interesting and delicious results.

Sun tea does not keep as long as boiled and brewed tea; the shelf life is about a day or so.

Sweet Tea Sorbet

When the heat has you wilting like a hydrangea in the midday sun, this divine Southern delicacy should chill you down and refresh your spirit. Dessert, pre-dinner lagniappe, coffee or tea accoutrement or palate cleanser, this little dish is just lovely.

Makes about 3 cups

1 family-size tea bag

3 cups boiling water

2 cups sugar

1 bunch fresh mint leaves

Juice of 2 lemons (about ¹/2 cup)

Recipe from the blog The Runaway Spoon; she's a dear friend.

Place the tea bag in a four-cup glass measuring bowl. Pour boiling water over and leave to steep until the tea is a dark amber color. You need a nice dark tea to get the flavor, a little darker than if you were drinking it straight up.

Pour 2 cups of the brewed tea into a saucepan with the sugar. Bring to a boil over medium heat, stirring to dissolve the sugar. Boil for 1 minute, then remove from the heat and drop in the mint leaves. Leave to cool and infuse.

When the sugar syrup is cool, strain out the mint leaves and pour into the measuring jug or bowl with the remaining 1 cup brewed tea. Stir in the lemon juice.

Pour the tea mix into the bowl of an ice cream maker and freeze according to the manufacturer's directions until the sorbet is light brown and grainy. This will likely take 30–40 minutes. Scoop the sorbet into a flat freezer container and freeze at least 8 hours, or overnight. Serve in chilled glasses.

Watermelon Sweet Tea

Sweet tea and watermelon—summertime staples. This brewed concoction featuring two of summer's most refreshing flavors is highlighted with a hint of mint—mint that in the sweltering summer heat is as evasive as can be. Garner as much as you can grab from the garden or your favorite farm stand and enjoy this delicious summer treat.

Makes 10 cups

1 family-size tea bag (I prefer Lipton)

5–6 leafy mint stems, divided

7 cups boiling water

3 pounds watermelon, seedless or seeds removed

Mint Simple Syrup (see page 6)

Ice

Place the tea bag and 3–4 mint stems in a large pitcher. Pour over the boiling water and allow to steep for 8–10 minutes, until the tea is a dark amber color. Remove and discard the tea bag and mint. Leave to cool.

Meanwhile, cut the watermelon flesh into chunks and puree in a blender until smooth. You may need to add a little water to get things moving. Pour the puree into a strainer set over a bowl and gently work the pulp to release the juice. Don't scrape and push too hard, or your tea will be too pulpy. You should have about 3 cups of juice. Refrigerate the juice until the tea is cooled.

In a pitcher or jug big enough to handle all the tea, combine the tea and watermelon juice and stir well. Stir in Mint Simple Syrup to taste; depending on the sweetness of the watermelon. Remember, you want it a little sweeter in the pitcher, because the ice will dilute it a bit. Serve over lots of ice with a sprig of mint for garnish.

❈ Sweet Tea Southern Sangria ❈

The house wine of the South, sweet tea is thus the base for this "sangria." Taking a batch of Farmer's Tea, Sun Tea, herbal tea, or your favorite fruit tea and infusing it with Southern summer fruits makes a gorgeous drink for all. Tangs and sweets, florals and herbals, and aesthetics with delicious tastes to boot all meld together for this drink—perfectly at home on your porch, piazza or veranda. Gather up a group of friends or family, or have a solo splurge and enjoy a glass.

Makes about 1 gallon

1-gallon batch Farmer's Tea
   or your favorite tea
4 peaches, pitted and sliced into wedges
4 plums, pitted and sliced into wedges
2 limes, sliced into rounds
2 lemons, sliced into rounds
1 large or two small oranges,
   sliced into rounds
Handful of cherries
Handful of raspberries
Handful of blackberries
Splash of mint, rosemary, lavender,
   or ginger Simple Syrup to
   taste* (see pages 6–7)

* 1/2 cup for the whole batch, or serve in a small pitcher for individual servings.

Fill a large pitcher with tea and add all the fruits. Add the flavored syrup of your liking and stir to mix. Serve over ice or chilled right out of the fridge. The longer it sits, the more infusion of fruit flavor the tea takes on. Good for a couple of days in the refrigerator, but I doubt you'll have much left when your crowd downs this one! Enjoy!

❋ Café au Lait a la DuPre ❋

I love the smell of coffee brewing. Bacon frying, bread baking, tea steeping—some smells are nostalgic reminders of a homey kitchen. Akin to tea, coffee has many different varieties and combos, but the basics are often the best.

Coffee and chocolate are no secret duo, but a duo nonetheless worth boasting. Whether as a drink or ingredients in my favorite chocolate cake, coffee and chocolate are a dynamo team.

This drink is from my design associate Laura DuPre Sexton's recipe cache. She's served this, as have her parents, for many a gathering, and I'm grateful to have been a guest of theirs and experienced this pleasant brew.

Serve over ice and you have an iced coffee drink worthy of any occasion. Au lait? *Oh yeah!*

Makes 1 pot

Pot of strong coffee

Sugar or sweetener to taste

2 tablespoons cocoa powder per 6 cups coffee

Milk or cream

Brew a pot of your favorite coffee extra strong. Sweeten to taste while warm so the sugar will dissolve, and add 2 tablespoons of cocoa powder for every 6 cups of coffee. Stir the sugar and cocoa until dissolved. Chill overnight or for the day if you make your coffee in the morning. At serving time, pour the cocoa-imbued coffee into serving glasses or mugs and lace with milk or cream. Whipped cream for topping is completely called for, and a serving of chocolate in the form of cake or tiramisu is in order with this lineup.

Basic Chocolate Cake

I nearly always substitute buttermilk for milk in batters (pancakes, other cakes, etc.), even in scrambled eggs. Since chocolate's natural flavor is enhanced by coffee, I use one cup of hot coffee in the batter as well.

Serves 12–16

2 cups sugar

1 3/4 cups all-purpose flour, sifted

3/4 cup cocoa powder

1 1/2 teaspoons baking powder

1 1/2 teaspoons baking soda

1 teaspoon salt

2 eggs, room temperature

1 cup buttermilk (shaken, not stirred)

1/2 cup vegetable oil

2 teaspoons vanilla extract

1 cup hot coffee

Preheat oven to 350 degrees F. Grease and flour two 9-inch round baking pans.

Combine all the dry ingredients, except coffee, in a large bowl. Add wet ingredients and beat together for 2 minutes. (Sample the batter before you add the coffee). Add coffee and mix until incorporated; the batter will be thin. (Try the batter now; the chocolate flavor has intensified.)

Divide the batter between the two pans and bake about 30 minutes, until a toothpick inserted in the center comes out clean. Allow the cakes to cool for about 10 minutes and then remove from the pans. Cool completely. Frost with the icing of your choice. Cookies and Cream Icing is one of my favorites.

❧ Baboo's Tea Cakes ❧

If Hawkinsville had a queen, Mrs. Barbara would be she. Affectionately known as Baboo by her beloved grandchildren, there was hardly a lady ever more regal, lovely, kind and classy as Mrs. Barbara. Her tea cakes were served at many an event in town and became as legendary as the dear doyenne herself. Whether serving with tea, at a ladies luncheon or shower, or simply sharing with friends, these Southern staples descended from true British roots with a pedigree and grace reminiscent of the lady who coined them.

It is with much honor and gratitude for sharing the recipe with me, that I now share it with you.

Makes about 24 cakes

2 sticks butter, softened

1 1/2 cups sugar

2 1/2 cups self-rising flour

1 egg, beaten

1 teaspoon vanilla

Preheat oven to 350 degrees F.

With a mixer, beat the butter then add the sugar and beat well. Add flour slowly, mixing with butter and sugar. Fold in the egg and vanilla until incorporated. Refrigerate dough for 30 minutes. Shape into 1 1/2-inch round balls (or roll out and use cookie cutters); place on a greased baking sheet. Bake for 10–15 minutes, or until edges are golden.

Citrus & Nectars

❋ *Mama Temple* ❋

The iconic, classic drink Shirley Temple, with its pinky hues, is reminiscent of the child star herself. Children especially are delighted to experience this bubbly drink of drinks. Lemon-lime soda, cherry juice or syrup, and a fun garnish are the classic combo. But I know one adult who relishes a Shirley Temple with a twist—my mama. A twist of fresh juices makes this classic a fun and fizzy treat on a hot day, at a festive event, or just for kicks.

Mama loves to serve this to a gaggle of gals, enjoy it as a single serving, or imbibe with my sisters for a girls' delight. The fresh juices awaken the flavors in the soda and cut the sweetness. Jarred or fresh cherries are just fine — Mama likes cherries of all sorts.

Makes about 4 cups

1 liter lemon-lime soda, divided

Juice of 2 lemons

Juice of 2 limes

¼ cup grenadine*

About 12 fresh cherries, pitted if you prefer

*Pomegranate juice or cranberry/pomegranate works just fine too.

In a pitcher, combine half of the soda, lemon and lime juices, grenadine and fresh whole cherries. Stir well and serve over ice. A bowl of cherries, lemons, and limes nearby adds additional garnish and fruit for more juice. Once consumed, use the remaining half liter and juice from garnishes for another round, or keep for the next day.

Ambrosia Nectar with Coconut Rim ❦

If the residents of Mt. Olympus feasted on ambrosia and nectar, then they were feasting on a delicacy of divinity indeed! Ambrosia is one of those dishes I look forward to with great zeal, for when citrus season comes in from our neighboring state to the south, I know that my treasured citrus salad is at hand. California and Texas, too, have fabulous citrus crops, and I take great pride in mixing different types of fresh citrus ambrosias. Of course, when someone else makes it, it always tastes better.

For instance, Mimi and Mrs. Mary made this for us from Thanksgiving through the holidays and into winter. Mimi said I didn't eat my ambrosia bur rather drank it! The nectar and juices in the bottom of the bowl was the best part to me, with all the fruit flavors infused together. I'm a bit of an ambrosia purist, preferring juicy sweet oranges, coconut, and some pomegranate arils for pizzazz. Fresh-squeezed orange juice makes all the difference here.

Makes about 4 cups

2 cups fresh-squeezed orange juice

1 cup pineapple with juice

1/2 cup pure pomegranate juice

**1 cup sweetened shredded coconut,
    plus more for rimming the glasses**

Ice

Pomegranate arils for garnish, optional

BLOOD ORANGES, *grapefruit, kumquats—whatever your favorite citrus—can be mixed in with this drink or your own version of ambrosia. The jewel-toned flesh of citrus, and even some pineapple chunks, is elegant for a dinner party, a morning treat, or a New Year's side.*

In a medium saucepan over medium-high heat, bring the mixed juices to a simmer and add the coconut. Allow to infuse and steep for about 5 minutes. Chill and then serve chilled or over ice.

To rim a glass with coconut, finely chop the shredded coconut and place on a small plate. On another small plate, squeeze out a couple tablespoons of fresh orange juice. Dip the rim of the glass in the juice and then the coconut, repeating if necessary until the rim is coated. Repeat with other glasses. Drop a few pomegranate arils into each glass, if desired.

❋ *Apricot Velvet* ❋

If ever a name was more apropos than this drink's name, I could scarce believe it so. Apricots are velvety by nature—smooth and soft yet lush, like fine velvet. Take their nectar, some of their preserves, a splash of almond and vanilla ice cream, and you have the makings for a velvet among velvets in the drink world.

Though other fruits can be used to create a similar drink, there is hardly a substitute for the sweet goodness the apricot brings to this beverage. Perfect as a dessert drink, an appetizer drink, or just a little something special.

Makes 2 servings

2 cups apricot nectar

3 tablespoons apricot preserves
   or 3 tablespoons honey
   and apricot puree

1/2 teaspoon almond extract

2 scoops (about 1 heaping cup)
   vanilla ice cream

Ice, optional

Dried apricots for garnish

Blend all the ingredients together and serve. Blending in ice makes the drink frothier and colder. Dried apricot kabobs make lovely garnishes and treats as well.

❋ *Mobile Mary Tomato Nectar* ❋

I have many fond memories of Mobile Bay, Alabama, and garden produce. Some of the best tomatoes come from here and also the Carolina Lowcountry. So what better way to combine the memories of the Bay and coast than as a memorable drink?

Old Bay Seasoning reminds me of seafood and summertime. It's a delicious enhancement for this tomato drink. Try pairing a Mobile Mary with crab cakes, grilled shrimp, or catfish, and think of serving it with your next Lowcountry boil.

Makes 2 servings

2 small garden tomatoes

¹/₂–1 small garden cucumber

4 large or 6 small basil leaves

2 sprigs thyme

1 tablespoon chopped rosemary leaves

1 teaspoon Old Bay Seasoning

Salt to taste

Cracked black pepper to taste

2 cups tomato juice* ¹/₂ cup ice
   (if you want it slushy)

*Add more liquid if you want to pour this drink over ice.

Blend the tomatoes, cucumber, herbs, spices, salt, and pepper until smooth, about 10 seconds. Add juice and ice and mix well. Rim your glasses in Old Bay, pour in the beverage, and garnish with a skewer of pickled okra and plum tomato wedges—or serve them on the side.

To kick this drink up a notch, try adding some Vidalia onion, shallot, or even a bit of garlic.

❉ *Lavender Limeade* ❉

A twist on a classic. Lavender has such a fantastic bouquet and flavor, blending well with many dishes. Lavender ice cream, lavender milk, or my Lavender Limeade will surely hit the spot any day. Plus, lavender and green look so beautiful together, this drink is fun to garnish and set in a tableaux.

Makes about 14 cups

6 heaping teaspoons lavender

12 cups water, divided

2–3 cups sugar, depending on your sweet tooth

1 1/2 cups freshly squeezed lime juice

1/2 teaspoon salt

Lavender sprigs for garnish

Lime slices for garnish

Mix lavender, 3 cups water, and sugar to taste in a saucepan. Boil gently for 5 minutes.

Strain out the lavender and add the now lavender-infused simple syrup mixture to 9 cups of water, lime juice, and salt. Mix well and serve ice cold. Garnish with lavender sprigs and sliced lime.

Mango Lassi, Y'all *

How to describe the luscious color of this drink? A pale salmon with rosy hues meets a shimmery goldfish but pales in comparison. Such a lovely color for such a lovely drink!

A lassi is a popular yogurt-based drink from the Indian subcontinent. With a tropical climate and tropical fruits at hand, the mango is a natural choice for this Punjabi drink. Bananas, too, find their way into lassi drinks, along with pinches of spice and other flavorings found in India.

Having tried this drink with peaches and other soft-fleshed fruits, I've found the mango lassi is truly memorable; the floral scent and delicious taste of the mango pair very well with rich yogurt. An accent of a peach and peach juice tends to meld this drink to the South.

While on the topic of yogurt, kefir, the "champagne of yogurts," is a splendid choice for this drink. It is smooth with a bit of effervescence from one of the cultures, and this little note of bubbly makes the drink truly great. Enjoy a lassi soon and bring a taste of Indian culture to your table.

Makes about 8 cups

3 cups diced fresh or frozen mango

1 cup peach nectar*

Small pinch of cinnamon

2 tablespoons Ginger Simple
   Syrup (see page 7)

1 tablespoon honey

3 cups kefir or plain yogurt

1 cup ice

Process half of all the ingredients together in a food processor or blender until well blended, scraping the sides as needed.

Repeat the blending process with the remaining half of the ingredients until blended smoothly. Blend again with ice for a cold smoothie.

*Apricot nectar or orange juice works as well.

ARE YOU A MARY ANN OR A GINGER?

When it comes to lemonade, are you a traditionalist clad in gingham, preferring the classic recipe? Or are you a bit saucier, preferring a twist on tradition and a more spice to life? Well, there is nothing wrong with either. But when it comes to lemonade, one of the gals' personas from Gilligan's Island may reflect your choice for this beverage.

Lemon juice and sugar served ice cold on a hot summer day: there is hardly anything better. Good old-fashioned lemonade is like Mary Ann, the "girl next door."

A Ginger preference for lemonade can be fun! Same premise and principle as for a Mary Ann—lemon juice and sugar, but livened up with some raspberry juice and ginger-infused simple syrup. Ginger has a lemony bite and marvelous bouquet. This amazing combo of ginger syrup with the lemons and sugar and raspberries plays on the palate like a movie star on the screen. This drink deserves an Oscar, so dress it up with a beautiful glass.

Why not invite the rest of the castaways for some lemonade goodness?

❋ *Mary Ann, or Traditional Lemonade* ❋

Makes about 14 cups

12 cups water, divided

2–3 cups sugar, depending
 on your sweet tooth

1 ¹/₂ cups freshly squeezed lemon juice

¹/₂ teaspoon salt

Ice

Lemon slices for garnish

Mix 3 cups water with sugar in a saucepan and boil gently for 5 minutes to make a simple syrup. In a pitcher, mix the remaining water, lemon juice, and salt. Mix in the simple syrup and serve ice cold. Garnish glasses with a slice of lemon.

❋ *Ginger Pink Lemonade* ❋

Makes about 1 gallon

12 cups water, divided

1 cup sugar, more or less, depending
   on your sweet tooth

1 cup Ginger Simple Syrup (see page 7)

1 1/2 cups freshly squeezed lemon juice

1 1/2 cups raspberry juice or

   1/2 cup raspberry puree

1/2 teaspoon salt

Candied ginger for garnish, optional

Raspberries for garnish, optional

Lemon slices for garnish, optional

Mix 3 cups of water and sugar to taste in a saucepan; boil gently for 5 minutes. In a separate container, pour the remaining 9 cups water, lemon juice, raspberry juice or puree, and salt. Add the Ginger Simple Syrup and mix well. Serve ice cold. Garnish with candied ginger, raspberries, or lemons.

Orange Spooner

Some drinks are just good: some drinks are good stories with provenance. Some drinks are all of these!

My Mimi's people are from the southwest corner of Georgia. Many of the Bainbridge cookbooks are part of my treasured library of culinary literature. Mimi loves to read them and be reminded of all the loved ones she knew growing up and the delicacies they served from their sideboards.

When I went to Auburn, I met a guy with the last name of Spooner. One weekend, this chap was brave enough to come home and eat Sunday dinner with my family. Immediately, my Grandmother Mimi was enthralled with Stephen's surname, for her grandparents were best of friends with the Spooners from Donaldsonville, not far from Bainbridge.

Amazing how the generations before us were so close. Who would have ever thought that my friend Steve would be a descendent of those Spooners my grandmother knew? His father's family is from the town, and his grandparents live there still. As for the drink part of this tale, one of Mimi's old cookbooks from her family's neck of the woods has a drink I love called an Orange Spooner. A good drink with a good name that I love to share with my Spooner friends—Stephen and his wife, Sarah Barry, and their baby Spooners, who have dubbed me Uncle James. I can't help but wonder if my family and Stephen's family ever had this drink together. I like to think so!

Makes about 4 cups

2 cups orange juice

Thin strip lime rind

¼ cup confectioners' sugar

2 sprigs mint

3 cups crushed ice

Place all ingredients, except ice, in a blender. Cover and blend for 10 seconds. Add crushed ice and blend until smooth. Serve with spoons if need be. Maybe that's where the name comes from? Enjoy!

Mrs. Wilson's Rosemary Lemonade

Bartender says, "What will you have, sir?"

"I'll have Mrs. Wilson's Rosemary Lemonade, please, or a 'James Farmer,'" my good man.

My house wine is sweat tea, but there are a couple of concoctions I simply relish just as much. One is Mrs. Wilson's Rosemary Lemonade and the other, a "James Farmer"—this Farmer's version of an Arnold Palmer.

Now, lemonade in the winter you ask? Yes sir, yes ma'am! Lemons are coming in as a winter crop from Florida and California, and what better time to enjoy their nectar than with one of winter's mainstay herbs in the Deep South. Of course, I enjoy this beverage any time of year, but there is just something luxurious about this brew in the depth of winter. It is actually good warm or cold, thus the basis of its year-round appeal.

Makes nearly 1 gallon

6 heaping teaspoons rosemary leaves

12 cups water, divided

2–3 cups sugar, more or less
  depending on your sweet tooth

1 1/2 cups freshly squeezed lemon juice

1/2 teaspoon salt

Sliced lemons for garnish

Rosemary sprigs for garnish

Mix rosemary, 3 cups water, and sugar in a saucepan and boil gently for 5 minutes.

Strain out the rosemary and add the now rosemary-infused simple syrup mixture to the remaining 9 cups water; add lemon juice, and salt. Mix well and serve ice cold. Garnish with sliced lemon and rosemary sprigs.

Here now is the story, morning-glory, of Mrs. Wilson's Rosemary Lemonade:

Dear friends of mine in Montgomery host me and "put me up" (or more so put up with me) when I'm staying in said town for the night, and Mrs. Wilson, a fabulous cook and hostess in her own right, often makes a batch of this delicious drink. I cannot be more thrilled to partake. Following her model, I have served this sweet, tangy and savory blend to family and party guests, and it is always received with smiles and requests for more.

Mrs. Wilson serves hers from beautiful antique crockery pitchers, thus making it taste that much better, in my humble opinion. A farm girl, originally from Opp, Alabama, Mrs. Wilson knows the importance of serving the best to friends and family. Often times the best is just simple yet elegant creations direct from the garden and the land. Rosemary lemonade epitomizes this—fresh herbs from the garden, juice right from lemons, and simple syrup to bring it all together. Mix this lemonade with my sweet tea, and you have one heck of an Arnold Palmer. Delicious and divine my friends, delicious and divine. Yeah, though, this Farmer does make a version of the famed beverage . . . selfishly dubbed a "James Farmer" (see page 14).

Fizzes & Sparklers

Indian Summer Apple-Ginger Sparkler

When apples are rolling in from Georgia's orchards, this fizzy drink makes for a cool refreshment on a warm Indian summer day. After the first frost of autumn, our southern climate often experiences warm days reminiscent of summertime, along with crisp nights and early mornings before the onset of winter proper. I love this time of year.

This drink is reflective of the temperature, for if the day has a briskness in the air, then you can serve it at room temperature. If it is a truly warm Indian summer day, then serve it over ice. Cinnamon sticks and candied ginger make for lovely garnishes, and the ginger is a delightful snack too.

Serves 6

¾ cup Ginger Simple Syrup (see page 7)

5 cups good apple cider

1 can ginger ale*

Cinnamon sticks for garnish

Candied ginger for garnish

*You can substitute sparkling cider for the ginger ale, if desired, or even sparkling mineral water for a less sweet drink.

Place 2 tablespoons syrup in each of 6 glasses. Optionally, freeze the syrup ahead to make ice cubes and place 2 ice cubes in each glass. Fill the glasses with regular ice cubes.

Mix the cider and ginger ale and pour over the ice. Stir to blend and chill the liquid. Garnish with cinnamon sticks and candied ginger.

Fizzes & Sparklers

Blackberry Fizz

A poem by Seamus Heaney called "Blackberry Picking" has intrigued me since I first read it in high school. I identified with the author when he wrote, "Our hands were peppered / With thorn pricks, our palms sticky as Bluebeard's . . . ," for I've had those peppered, sticky hands and the pricks of thorns amid a blackberry bramble.

My sisters and I would pile high our hoards of deep aubergine blackberries as we picked, knowing we would be trading them in for blackberry pies, tarts, cobblers and a fun drink. Salut to blackberry picking, to their growing wild on the fences on the farm or waiting ripe for the taking right off your favorite market shelves.

Serves 4

4 thick stems rosemary

2 pint cups fresh blackberries

Juice of ¹/₂ lemon

Juice of ¹/₂ lime

2 cans ginger ale

**Rosemary and Ginger Simple
    Syrups, optional (see page 7)**

FOR ADDED DELIGHT, serve Deep Dish
Blackberry Tart (see page 50).

Remove the leaves from the rosemary stems to within 1 inch of the top. Skewer 3–4 blackberries onto each naked stem and set aside. Puree the remaining blackberries with the lemon and lime juices.

Pour the ginger ale into a carafe and infuse with about 2 tablespoons each of Ginger and Rosemary Simple Syrup, if desired, for additional sweetness.

Divide blackberry puree among 4 glasses and finish filling with infused ginger ale. Garnish each glass with a skewer of blackberries.

Deep Dish Blackberry Tart

Using a deep dish allows you to fill the tart chock full of the rich colors and flavors that blackberries provide. Use extra dough to make a lattice or leaves for the top of the tart.

Makes 1 (9-inch) round tart

TART DOUGH

2 cups all-purpose flour

1/2 teaspoon salt

1 tablespoon sugar

3/4 cup (1 1/2 sticks) cold butter

1/2 cup ice water

Combine the dry ingredients with your fingers in a large mixing bowl. If using a food processor, pulse to mix.

Slice the butter into cubes and mix into the dry ingredients using a hand mixer, or pulse in food processor, until the dough begins to clump into a ball and the butter is pea size or smaller. Pour the water into the mixture slowly, continuing to mix until the dough comes together in a ball.

On a floured surface, roll the dough into a large "pat." Wrap it in plastic and chill in the refrigerator for about 1 hour. After the dough is chilled, press it into the bottom and all the way up the sides of a 9-inch round tart pan using your fingers. The rustic look of an imperfect crust is what makes the simple elegance of this dessert so pretty.

BLACKBERRY FILLING

1 1/2 cups fresh blackberries

1/4 cup vanilla sugar (see page 85)

Blackberry jam for glaze and garnish*

Whipped Vanilla Crème Fraîche
   (see page 85)

*Substitute peach or apricot jam for a clearer glaze.

Preheat oven to 350 degrees. Fill the tart shell with blackberries and sprinkle with vanilla sugar. Cover tart with strips or cutout shapes of dough. Bake about 45 minutes, or until the dough is golden brown. Glaze with heated blackberry jam and serve with whipped cream and a dollop of jam on the side as well.

Sparkling Grapefruit Drink

There are some colors in nature that are simply spellbinding. The inside of a red grapefruit—that salmon/coral/pink/creamy orange is so gorgeous! Any opportunity to show off this hue is an honor.

Grapefruit has a distinct flavor that I find most folks either love or hate. Like most produce, a perfectly ripe grapefruit is utterly fantastic. I love pairing this flavor with rosemary, lavender or ginger. With such a spectacular color, a little razzle-dazzle is completely fine, so a splash of ginger ale with one of the aforementioned herbs or ginger syrups is so appealing to the senses—beautiful to the eyes, lovely to smell and delicious to taste. It can be doubled, tripled or whatever for a scrumptious punch as well.

Makes about 12 cups

2 quarts grapefruit juice (fresh is great but good-quality is just fine)

1 liter ginger ale

1 cup Rosemary, Lavender, or Ginger Simple Syrup (see Herbal Simple Syrup, page 6)

1 whole grapefruit

To the juice, add the syrup of your liking. Stir and then add the ginger ale. Slice the grapefruit into rounds and float in a punch bowl. Serve chilled or over ice.

Fizzes & Sparklers

❧ *Peach Julep* ❧

Julep cups, starched linen napkins and peaches—iconic Southern staples for entertaining, porch sitting, or savoring a summer afternoon. Drinking out of silver, pewter and the like is an experience unlike any other, for the metal vessels take on the temperature of their holdings and give not only our palates a pleasing wash but our lips a cold touch. A silver tray full of these refreshing blends of summer's produce and garden goodness beckons your guests to take one and toast to all that is good and lovely. Fizzy or flat, invigorating and visually enticing, the chemistry of warm air meeting cold liquid creates a luscious layer of condensation on the julep cup that is just impossible to resist. Serve your Peach Juleps with cocktail napkins or fun linens and let the celebration of summer begin!

Makes 1 pitcher of juleps

10 mint leaves

1 tablespoon sugar

2 cups peach nectar

1 cup unsweetened tea

1/4 cup Basic Simple Syrup (see page 5)
   or Mint Simple Syrup (see page 6)

1 cup sparkling mineral water
   or plain sparkling water

Crushed ice

Peach wedges and mint
   leaves for garnish

Muddle the mint leaves and sugar in the bottom of a julep pitcher. Pour in the nectar, tea, and syrup and give it a good stir.

Add the sparkling water and gently stir again. Pour over crushed iced into julep cups. Garnish with peach wedges and mint leaves.

FOR A SANS SUDS JULEP, just use a cup of water or double the tea. For a ginger-infused julep, substitute the tea and sparkling water for ginger ale and the mint syrup for ginger syrup. Ginger is fantastic with peaches and muddled mint!

❉ *White Peach Slush* ❉

White peaches are precious jewels of the summer peach season. It's not a long season for these delectable delights, but whenever they are available, I sure enjoy every bite, or sip, I can.

With a perfume as delicious as their flavor, these peaches make for magnificent additions or center-stage options for desserts, salads, fruits dishes and drinks. Since I often find white peaches to be a bit soft (their shelf life is not the longest), I love to puree them with some thyme-infused brown sugar syrup. Thyme, especially lemon thyme, pairs so well with these peaches, you'll wonder how you ever made it this far without the two! Pouring this concoction over ice is a celebration of the season, while blending the ice right into the drink makes a luscious slush. Take your pick for this peachy treat. More fun awaits with a splash of sparkling water!

Serves 4

3–4 peeled white peaches

3–4 tablespoons Lemon Thyme–
    Infused Brown Sugar Simple
    Syrup (see page 7)

¼ teaspoon almond extract

2 cups peach nectar

1 cup sparkling water, or
    more for extra fizz

Ice

Chopped dried apricots for garnish

Chopped almonds for garnish

Thyme sprigs for garnish

Peel the peaches and puree with the syrup, almond extract, and nectar. Don't hesitate to add a splash or two more of nectar if the peach puree doesn't yield the desired amount of liquid.

Divide the puree mixture into glasses and pour sparkling water over. Stir well and ice down if desired, or blend plenty of ice right in to make a slush. Serve with apricots, almonds, and thyme sprigs for garnish.

Cordials & Punches

❋ Pear-Apple Slush ❋

From the first bite into one of these crispy fruits, the flavor of true apple or pear decadence begins to descend upon the taste buds. Tart, sweet, mild, and sharp—there is an apple and a pear for every preference. Freezing this drink simply revs up the flavor and texture in a cold-elicious slush.

This drink can be mimicked with other juices and seasonal fruits, but the apple and pear are very complementary and make a refreshing combo.

Serves 4

4 cups high-quality apple juice or cider

1 1/2 cups pear nectar

1 apple or pear for garnish

Honey or Herbal Simple Syrup

to taste (see page 6)*

Sparkling water

*Freezing separates the water and fruit sugars, making the juice a bit less sweet. Add honey or simple syrup to sweeten to your liking before freezing.

Pour the fruit juices into a shallow dish or pan that can be frozen, and chill in the freezer until a slushy ring or band begins to form around the edge. Don't let it freeze completely.

Break up the frozen juice with a fork, scraping the slush to the center of the pan; then freeze again for 1 hour, or until slushy once more. Using a fork, break up the frozen juices.

Scoop out the slush four glasses. Add the wedge of apple or pear or both. Top off with sparkling water and serve.

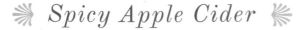

Spicy Apple Cider

Every year, apples from the northern mountain orchards of Georgia start coming in, giving us fabulous fruits for a season. Pies, cakes, tarts, butter, and sauce all come from the apple crop, but one apple product in particular is congenial with the crisp autumn days—apple cider.

Velvety smooth, delightful to the taste, and luscious warm or chilled, apple cider is made by concentrating apple juice with flavors oh so complementary: cinnamon, cloves, brown sugar, and a dash of citrus. In lieu of trekking to the mountain orchards and bringing home a jug or two of this delectable nectar, this recipe is a delicious consolation. I hope you enjoy it.

Makes 8 cups

½ **gallon good-quality apple juice, such as Simply Apple**

3 **tablespoons fresh-squeezed lemon or orange juice**

3 **cinnamon sticks**

1 **dozen whole cloves**

1 **cup Rosemary Simple Syrup (see Herbal Simple Syrup, page 6)**

Cinnamon sticks for garnish, optional

Cinnamon sugar for garnish, optional

Simmer the juices, cinnamon, and cloves together until bubbles appear. Add the rosemary syrup and stir. Serve warm or chilled.

This cider is happy to stay on low heat and be dipped into throughout the day. Garnish with cinnamon sticks if you wish, or rim your glasses with cinnamon sugar.

Berried Treasure

Cranberries and raspberries tote the regal glow of rubies and garnets and jewel tones in between. From the richness of these colors comes a treasure of health benefits to boot. The vitamins and nutrients associated with these superfruits are astounding.

This concoction of red jewels is a play on seasons as well, making this potion of "berried treasure" that much more desirable. Typically, cranberries are autumn/winter fruits while raspberries grow in the summer. Since the two aren't seasonal together, using frozen raspberries is the trick to making this drink frothy and cold. A dose of raspberry preserves highlights the floral notes of the raspberry and pairs delightfully with the tartness of the cranberry.

Toast the allure of buried treasure with a glass of Berried Treasure, and receive an extra dose of health and happiness!

Makes 2 tall glasses and bit more

2 cups fresh cranberries

2 cups frozen raspberries

3–4 tablespoons raspberry jam or berry conserve

Cranberry or raspberry juice*

Sparkling mineral water, optional

Berries for garnish

Mint for garnish

In a juicer, push all the cranberries through, followed by the jam or conserve and the raspberries. Pour the juice into glasses and top off with sparkling water if desired. Garnish with berries and mint.

*For kitchens sans juicers, blend the berries and jam together until smooth. Spoon the blended concoction on top of cranberry or raspberry juice in the glass, and garnish.

Blueberry Oatmeal Drink

This twist on a classic breakfast parfait will surely get your day started in the right direction and keep you full and energized throughout the morning, or refresh your outlook anytime of day. Though made with blueberries, this drink/dish can be served with your favorite seasonal berry or berry blend. From strawberries, to currants, to raspberries and blackberries, this oatmeal blended beverage is hearty, healthy and very tasty.

My family often had this with blackberries, which rambled wildly along many of the fencerows. For additional crunch, toasted pecans, walnuts or almonds can be served atop the drink or as side stash.

Serves 2

3 tablespoons oatmeal

Pinch of salt

1 cup boiling water

1 scant cup blueberries

2 heaping teaspoons local honey

6 tablespoons plain Greek-
    style yogurt, divided

Berries, granola, or nuts for garnish

Spoon the oats into a heatproof bowl and mix with the salt. Cover with boiling water and allow to stand for about 10 minutes. Place the soaked oats in a blender with the berries, honey, and 4 tablespoons of yogurt. Blend well and scrape the sides of the blender as needed. Pour blended mixture into two glasses and swirl 1 tablespoon yogurt into each glass. Garnish with berries, granola, or nuts.

Variations You can mix the honey and yogurt together beforehand. Alternatively, use a splash of vanilla, a pinch of cinnamon, or a sprinkle of brown sugar to sweeten the yogurt. Other types of berries can be substituted for blueberries.

❊ *Blue Lagoon* ❊

Often during the summer, piles and pints of summer berries start rolling into the kitchen from the garden—my friends' gardens, my grandparents' garden, and even the roadside stashes of berries I keep my eyes peeled for this time of year. Whatever shall I do with all these berries?, I often ask, and then I remember a favorite drink—a Blue Lagoon.

Blueberries, strawberries, and blackberries (a scuppernong or muscadine or two don't hurt either) all combine to make a lagoon of refreshing berry juices..

If a juicer isn't in your kitchen arsenal, then puree the berries for a frothier drink. Whether in the peak of summer's heat or pulled from the freezer mid-winter, take a few handfuls of your favorite berries and dive into your own blue lagoon!

Serves 2–4

1 cup strawberries

1 cup blueberries

1 cup blackberries

Handful of scuppernongs or muscadines

Honey or sugar to taste (though often
   the berries are adequately sweet)

Juice the berries and sweeten to taste. Serve over ice. Optionally, puree the berries with sweetener of choice in a blender. Then add $1^1/_2$ cups ice and blend to make a smoothie.

Blue Boy/Blue Belle ❋

A superfruit chock full of antioxidants, nutrients, and vital elements for a healthy life, blueberries are simply delicious besides.

As a child, I relished the opportunity to pick blueberries, for I knew the reward would be a pie, a cake, jam, or some kind of blueberry treat. I loved to sprinkle them on my cereal or ice cream, which led to the creation of this drink. When the cereal was gone or the ice cream had melted, a blueberry or two would have seeped their nectar into the remaining milk and infused those last spoonfuls with divine flavor. Taking that same approach, this drink is sure to be a thrill for your boys and belles. They might like a slice of Brown Sugar Blueberry Pound Cake as well!

Makes 2 glasses

1 cup fresh blueberries

**1–2 tablespoons vanilla sugar
(see page 85)**

1 cup milk

¹/₂ cup heavy whipping cream

Puree the blueberries with the sugar and then incorporate them into the milk and cream, mixing well. Chill and serve.

BLEND ICE *into it for a smoothie effect.*

Cordials & Punches

Brown Sugar Blueberry Pound Cake

Serves 12–16

3 1/2 cups cake flour plus
   2 tablespoons, divided

1/2 teaspoon baking powder

1 cup (2 sticks) butter, softened

1/2 cup shortening

3 1/2 cups (1 pound) brown sugar

1/2 cup granulated sugar

1/2 cup vanilla sugar (see page 85)

5 eggs

1 cup buttermilk

1 teaspoon vanilla extract

1/2 teaspoon salt

1 1/2 cups fresh blueberries

Preheat oven to 300 degrees. Grease and flour a 10-inch Bundt pan or two small loaf pans.

Sift 3 1/2 cups flour and the baking powder into a bowl and set aside.

Using a mixer, cream the butter and shortening together in a large bowl. Add the sugars alternately and continue beating. Add the vanilla, then add eggs one at a time, incorporating well after each egg is added. Beginning and ending with the flour mixture, add the flour and milk to the creamed butter, sugar, and eggs.

Mix the blueberries with 2 tablespoons flour and gently fold them into the batter. If desired, you can leave off the extra flour and let the blueberries concentrate at the bottom of the cake.

Pour the batter into the prepared pan(s) and bake for 2 hours. Fair warning, your house will smell wonderful! Remove from oven and allow to cool. Serve with Whipped Vanilla Bean Crème Fraîche (page 85) and a jar of Blue Boys/ Blue Belles (facing).

❈ *Bluffton Peach* ❈

The South Carolina Lowcountry is a magical place full of history, gorgeous marsh vistas, and tradition. Palmetto Bluff is one of my favorite spots on earth. Since my sister and bother-in-law live in the nearby laid-back Lowcountry town of Bluffton, we enjoy this drink with peaches I bring them from home or some of South Carolina's own.

Peaches and basil are fabulous friends. I use them in salads together for a swimmingly delicious palate pleaser, and that same combo makes this drink memorable. My sweet basil syrup with peach nectar and puree, combined with your favorite tea, makes a drink worthy of savoring while on the May River. If you cannot make it to the May River to view the swaying palmetto fronds, smell the brackish water and air, and watch a Lowcountry sunrise through bangs of Spanish moss, then make a Bluffton Peach and it will take you there.

Serves 6

6 peaches, peeled, pitted, and pureed

3 cups peach nectar

1 cup Sweet Basil Simple Syrup (see
   Herbal Simple Syrup, page 6)

3 cups unsweetened Farmer's
   Tea (see page 10), green
   tea, or your favorite tea

Puree the peaches and mix the puree with the nectar, syrup, and tea. Serve chilled or over ice, with peach slices in the glasses for garnish. Basil leaves make a nice accent, too.

Farmer's Garden Wassail

Here We Come a Wassailing…

"… Among the leaves so green …
Love and joy come to you,
And to you your wassail too,
And God bless you and send you a happy New Year,
And God send you a happy New Year."

Makes 4 cups to be mixed into hot tea

4 cups water

2 small oranges sliced into rounds

2 bags Earl Grey Tea

2 tablespoons whole cloves

2 tablespoons ground cinnamon

3 small cinnamon sticks

2 stems rosemary

1 cluster juniper berries

Farmer's Tea (see page 10)

Combine all ingredients in a small to medium-size pot and simmer on low heat, stirring as you pass by the stove. Mix into a batch of sweetened Farmer's Tea. Chilled, this brew will last for a few days. Merry, merry!

Though I've never actually gone wassailing, I have made a batch of wassail to fill my home with the scents of the season and share with friends and family. My Farmer's Garden Wassail incorporates the garden and seasonal produce to pack your home with fragrance for days to come. I actually make two batches of this wassail: one for ingesting and one for scenting the home.

Wassailing is an act of celebrating—somewhat noisily—while drinking a concoction (wassail) of warm beer or wine seasoned with spices and fruit. An English tradition that was brought to the colonies, wassailing and making wassail became a source of delight, warmth, season's greetings, and entertainment for merry folk; and rightly so! A small pot, simple ingredients, and a few minutes—that's all one needs for wassail making. Stir the pot occasionally as it sits on low heat, gently simmering and perfuming your home with the aromas of its elements—oranges, cinnamon, cloves, tea, rosemary, and juniper: all are readily available from the garden and grocery.

Wassail is a perfect gift to give your neighbors, friends, and party hosts, and to send home as a favor from your own holiday bash. Add this batch to a batch of Farmer's Sweet Tea and you'll have your very own delicious Christmas cocktail—Arnold Palmer meets Santa!

❋ Georgia Sunrise ❋

Sunsets are fabulous and spellbinding, but a sunrise is a glorious, welcome start of a new day, Sunrises tear night's darkness with streams of red, orange, and yellow light, and these colors are caught in a drink I call a Georgia Sunrise. Sunrises are full of hope and promise, and I hope and promise you this drink will surely make the beginning of a new day simply marvelous. Might as well start breakfast with a peach tart as well! The breakfast of champions, I'm sure!

Makes about 4 cups

3 peaches, pitted and sliced into wedges
   (skin on or off, your preference)

2 cups peach nectar

1 cup cranberry juice

Puree the peaches in a blender. Pour in nectar and cranberry juice and mix well. Serve chilled or over ice.

Deep Dish Peach Tart

Serves 6–8

1/2 recipe Tart Dough (see page 50)

Brown Sugar Graham Cracker
    Crust (see below)

5–6 ripe peaches (1 reserved with skin on),
    peeled and chopped, about 2 cups

1/4 cup vanilla sugar (see page 85)

1/4 cup brown sugar

4 tablespoons peach or
    apricot jam for glaze

Whipped Vanilla Bean Crème
    Fraîche (see page 85)

Make the tart dough and let chill, then roll out and cut into strips to make a lattice crust. Prepare graham cracker crust.

Mix chopped peaches with sugars and then add peaches and sugar mixture to the crust. Top with lattice crust and bake for about 30 minutes, until lattice is golden and peaches are warm and bubbly. Glaze with jam that has been heated and slightly cooled. Serve with Whipped Vanilla Bean Crème Fraîche and reserved peach sliced into wedges.

BROWN SUGAR GRAHAM CRACKER CRUST

2 cups ground graham crackers

3 tablespoons dark brown sugar

1/4 teaspoon salt

1 stick unsalted butter, melted
    and slightly cooled

For the graham cracker crust, preheat oven to 350 degrees. Combine graham crackers, brown sugar, and salt in a bowl. Stir in melted butter. Press mixture into bottom and up sides of a small deep-dish tart pan, or a 9-inch metal pie pan is just fine too! Refrigerate until the crust is set, about 15–20 minutes. Bake until the crust is golden brown, about 15 minutes. Allow to cool.

Mayflower

Too much of a good thing is a really good thing, right? This drink is created for my sister Sarah Margaret, whom we called "Maggie May," in honor of the month she was born. May's drink of choice, a Mayflower, is a combo of good things she treasures, and I dare not say it's too much! Just the right amount of goodness mixed together for an absolutely lovely drink.

Playing off the colors of zinnias, hydrangeas, and even some poke sal, this Mayflower totes no Pilgrims but carries notes of sweet summer fruit juices and a garnish almost too pretty to eat. Do eat it, though, for the floral and fruit essences are simply delicious.

Serves 4

1 cup peach nectar

1 cup pineapple juice

1 cup cranberry juice

1 cup green tea

1/3 cup Rosemary Simple Syrup (see
    Herbal Simple Syrup, page 6)

Blackberries, peach wedges,
    pineapple chunks, and
    rosemary sprigs for garnish

Mix the juices, tea, and syrup together. Chill or serve over ice. Vintage tea towels and garden flowers make it all that more special and festive.

❋ *Honeysuckle Cordial* ❋

Recipe from my friend's blog, The Runaway Spoon. Smell is the direct sense linked to memory. I can smell honeysuckle and immediately be taken to my childhood farm in Middle Georgia. The smells of spring are a cacophony of scents, from the heaviest of florals—such as jasmine, privet, honeysuckle, magnolia, and gardenia—to the slightest of scents—such as roses, garden herbs, and fresh-cut grass.

This lovely cordial captures the scene of the season and makes a refreshing drink topped off with soda or tonic. Other delights: Honeysuckle Cordial to sweeten iced tea, or drizzle it over fresh summer fruit.

Makes about 2 cups

4 cups honeysuckle buds,
   lightly packed
1 lemon
2 cups sugar
2 cups boiling water
1 teaspoon citric acid*

*Citric acid is a natural preservative. It is also called sour salt and can be found in the kosher section at the grocery.

Gather the honeysuckle blossoms and shake them in a colander or lay them out on a tea towel. Pick through the blossoms, removing any green leaves, stems, brown, wilted buds, and bugs. Place the sorted blossoms in a large bowl.

Using a vegetable peeler, peel off strips of the lemon peel (no white pith) and place on top of the blossoms. Cut the lemon into slices; discard the stem ends, and drop the slices into the bowl. Toss to combine.

In a saucepan, bring the sugar and water to a boil, stirring to dissolve the sugar. Pour the boiling syrup over the blossoms and lemons in the bowl. Stir in the citric acid, cover the bowl with a tea towel, and leave undisturbed for 24 hours. The next day, strain the cordial through a sieve lined with cheesecloth into a large bowl or measuring jug with a pouring spout. Pour the strained cordial into bottles or jars.

❋ Pomegranate Cooler ❋

A superfruit, the pomegranate is prized for its levels of nutrients, antioxidants, vitamins, minerals, and all-around goodness. This fruit is not only phenomenal for the body but pleasing to the eye as well. Good-quality pomegranate juice spiked with a splash of lime juice makes for a cooler sort of drink worthy of partaking any time of day. Yet, an herbal kick makes this wonder fruit's juice come alive even more. As a starter, snack, power lunch, or dessert, this drink is sure to bring health to your home.

Serves 1–10

For every 1 cup of pomegranate juice, add 1 squeeze of a lime wedge.

For every cup, 1 teaspoon of an Herbal Simple Syrup for a garden tone (see page 6).

For a bit of bubbly, a splash or two of sparkling water is nice over ice and quite refreshing. Arils and lime wedges make lively and lovely garnishes.

Watermelon Punch

Though it's hotter than a pepper sprout down South in the summer, I gladly endure the heat to the avail of produce abounding. The heat only makes drinks like this Watermelon Punch—with its slushy, frothy, icy nature and cooling demeanor—that much more enjoyable.

Watermelon is delectably cool when chilled. And the color of this beverage is magnificent, I might say!

If by chance you're counting your calories, this one's for you. Hardly any at all, and the only sugar is the natural fructose from the juice. I hear the blender raring up—it must be Watermelon Punch time now!

Serves 2

Juice of one lime

1 cup good orange juice

About 4 cups watermelon chunks

Mint for garnish

Watermelon wedges for garnish

Into the blender container, pour the lime juice and orange juice; then fill the container with chunks of watermelon. Cover and blend the watermelon to a liquid. Fill the container again with the remaining watermelon and blend to liquefy. Pour over crushed ice, or blend ice into the drink for a slushy punch. Garnish each glass with mint or a watermelon wedge.

Birthday Party Punch ❧

Kids love this one! This punch is super for a crowd! What is it about fizz that makes kids lap up a punch? Grown-ups, too, love this, for it is easy to make. Serve this up at your next birthday out a galvanized bucket or big Mason jar, or ladle it out of toy buckets for, well, buckets of fun!

Serves 8

**4 cups good-quality grape juice
(white or red just fine)**

4 cups good-quality cran-grape juice

**24 apple juice ice cubes (100% pure
apple juice frozen in ice trays)**

**1 liter ginger ale, lemon-lime
soda, or sparkling water***

**1 big bunch (about 1 pound) seedless
red and green grapes, sliced in half**

3 oranges, sliced into rounds

*The soda, of course, will be sweeter; but the sparkling water, I feel, has just the right amount of fizz without the added sweetness.

Combine the juices into a large serving container and pour in the fizz of your choice. Add the apple juice ice cubes and float the sliced grapes and oranges in the punch or use for garnish.

❋ Frosted Orange Varsity Punch ❋

The Varsity is an institution in Atlanta for college students, midtown and downtown workers, tourists, and just about anyone else perusing, pausing in, or passing through Atlanta. Known for all sorts of dogs, burgers, fries, and onion rings, the Varsity is also known for its "Frosted Orange," akin to an Orange Julius (a rivalry over which came first is still ensuing).

The Varsity is known not only for its grub but also for its lingo: "What'll ya have! What'll ya have!" most noted as the greeting from your server. With a whole liturgy of expressions and shorthand, The Varsity will not disappoint as an entertainment venue, let alone a great spot for a "Sally Rand through the garden."

The Varsity's N.I. Orange (without ice) and F.O. (Frosted Orange shake) are the inspirations for this punch.

Serves 12–15

3 (6-ounce) cans frozen orange
    juice concentrate, thawed

3 cups milk

3 cups water

1 ¼ cups sugar or Basic Simple
    Syrup (see page 5)

3 teaspoons pure vanilla extract

36 orange juice ice cubes (good-
    quality OJ frozen in ice trays)

Divide the ingredients and process in thirds. In a blender, combine the orange juice, milk, water, sugar, and vanilla. Cover and blend until smooth. With blender running, add a third of the ice cubes, one at a time, through the opening in lid. Blend until smooth and pour into a punch bowl. Repeat the process twice. Serve immediately out of punch bowl.

Milky Concoctions

Rosemary and Pecan Crème de la Crème

This decadent drink is sublime on chilly autumn evenings and can warm up the frosty air on a dreary winter night. Here in the Deep South, rosemary is an evergreen herb, often used as shrub or backdrop for perennial borders. With a long, warm (pronounced HOT) growing season, our rosemary-flavored dishes and drinks often take center stage in the cooler months, when the frost has taken care of the tender herbs. Plus, pecans are a fall and winter crop for us, so this combo is only natural.

An old European adage states that "rosemary grows where strong women live," and this saying has been adopted into Southern culture as well. Whether at the home of the matriarch or the residence of a gaggle of strong-willed belles, you are sure to find the cream of the crop where that fantastic herb is growing. Toast these ladies with a Rosemary and Pecan Cream drink!

Serves 4

2 cups 2 percent or whole milk, divided

3–4 long sprigs fresh rosemary

12 pecan sandies or pecan shortbread
  cookies, plus more for serving

4 scoops good-quality vanilla ice
  cream or frozen vanilla custard

Sugared rosemary leaves for garnish

In a medium saucepan, gently bring 1 cup of milk to a boil with the rosemary, stirring frequently. Pour the rosemary-infused milk into a bowl and allow to cool for 10 minutes; then remove and discard the rosemary.

In a food processor or blender, blend the cookies and still-warm milk until smooth. Add the remaining 1 cup of milk during this process. Blend thoroughly.

Scoop the ice cream into the blender and blend until incorporated fully. Pour into glasses and serve with additional pecan sandies and sugared rosemary leaves.

❋ Coconut Cream and Pineapple Puree ❋

My sister Meredith loves the classic piña colada flavor of pineapple and coconut, which has been in vogue for many years. This blend of tastes has a kinship to one of her favorite desserts, which she also shares with her brother—coconut cream pie. This dessert drink of iconic flavors is one Mere and I make throughout the year. It is easy and quite delicious, fabulous warm or cold.

Serves 2

1 cup 2 percent milk

1 cup sweetened shredded coconut

1 teaspoon vanilla

2 tablespoons vanilla sugar (see
   page 85) or brown sugar

1 cup pineapple chunks

Pineapple wedges for garnish

On medium heat, bring the milk and coconut to a simmer. Add vanilla and sugar and stir constantly for 5 minutes. Remove from heat.

Puree the pineapple. Add the milk and coconut to the puree and blend together. Pour and serve frothy while still warm, or chill and serve with a straw. Pineapple wedges make perfect garnishes and can serve as tools to dip the last little bits out of the glass.

MRS. MCCALL'S
PIÑA COLADA CAKE

There is a great dessert that was the inspiration for this cake that I'm afraid I could eat my weight in, and probably have done over the years. It's the Piña Colada Cake at McCall's Tastes to Remember on Commercial Circle in Warner Robins, Georgia. Mrs. Karen McCall and her son Ken carry on the tradition of a quick, delicious lunch for the work crowd in an elegant fashion. Their sandwich shop sports the classics such as chicken salad, a Monte Cristo, a Reuben, pasta salad, and a myriad other soups de jour and desserts. If you can't get to Warner Robins, then my Coconut Cream and Pineapple Puree plays a good second fiddle to Mrs. Karen's Piña Colada Cake.

Farmer's Garden Mint Shake

With an abundance of mint or just a few sprigs, this herb can flavor and scent your kitchen in the best of ways. Spicing up a salad, garnishing a dish, and adding pizzazz to drinks are some of its all-around uses.

One thing I love about this shake is its versatility of preparation. Yogurt, ice cream, whipping cream, or milk—the drink can be made with any of these dairy products and is also fantastic with soy, almond, or even sweetened coconut milk.

With mint readily available in the garden during the warm growing seasons and also obtainable at markets and grocers nearly year-round, this drink can be served anytime. A twist of lime, lemon, or orange adds a kick of citrus enhancement. You're due for a mint shake real soon, between courses as a palate cleanser, as a light dessert, a fun breakfast, or a snack.

Serves 2

1 heaping cup fresh mint leaves,
   plus a couple for garnish

¼ cup Simple Syrup, Basic or Herbal,
   your choice (see page 5 or 6)

1 heaping cup yogurt or ice cream

1 cup whipping cream or whole milk

1 tablespoon freshly squeezed
   lemon, lime, or orange juice

1 teaspoon zest

1 ½ cups ice

Citrus rind or thin wedge for garnish

Blend all ingredients except ice until smooth and well combined. Add ice and blend again. The mixture will become frothy.

Pour into glasses and garnish with mint and citrus rinds. Enjoy this milkshake-turned-mintshake!

Whipped Vanilla Bean Crème Fraîche

It just amazes me how many things can come from milk. It's life's first beverage. It's a must on every trip to the grocery store. If you haven't hooked onto organic milk and cream yet, you are missing out. Lactose-free milk is about the best glass of anything you'll ever drink! I digress . . .

Whipped cream is simply divine. The science of physically changing a liquid into a solid is astounding, but what is so amazing to me is the taste. With a scant bit of sugar, some good vanilla, and the inside of a vanilla bean pod, you can have the best of dessert toppings in a matter of minutes.

I inherited my great-great aunt Irene's "whipper," a wiry paddle that takes the strongest of arms a long time to whip up a batch of this heavenly topping. Want a workout? Trust me, you'll burn off the calories you'll consume by whipping cream by hand.

There is a bit of an art to whipping cream. Here are a few tips and my recipe.

- *Use a metal, glass, or ceramic bowl. Plastic won't cut it.*
- *Always use cold cream and good vanilla beans and vanilla extract. This is one delicacy; you'll truly taste the vanilla and you want the best.*
- *Whip, mix, or whisk until the cream forms soft peaks and just looks right. It shouldn't be the least bit runny; it will get runny on a hot piece of pie, but that's perfectly apropos!*

Master this and you'll have so many friends and family wanting a finger-licking taste, you'll have to give out numbers!

**2 cups crème fraîche* or
heavy whipping cream**

1 tablespoon good vanilla

**1 scant teaspoon scraped
vanilla bean pod**

1 scant tablespoon vanilla sugar**

*Crème fraîche is more solid than whipping cream and wants a bit more sugar.

Beat until it begins to form soft peaks that can stand on their own and are no longer runny. Serve with just about anything and it will be delicious, I'm sure!

VANILLA SUGAR

Cutting up and placing a scraped vanilla bean pod into about 1 cup sugar will allow the vanilla flavor to infuse the sugar. There are other methods, but this is the one I use.

Promised Land

Whenever I heard stories in Sunday school about the Israelites journeying through the wilderness for forty years en route to the Promised Land, I always got thirsty hearing about the milk and honey they would have upon arrival. Those two promised delights might have me wandering for forty years, too.

One of Mimi's vintage cookbooks had a recipe for a warm milk drink that she prepared for me when I was a child. I have adapted it and relish it more so even today. This drink combines the best ingredients: organic milk and Savannah Bee Company honey. Take this drink to bed, savor it as a dessert, or let it start off your day in an excellent way. Good warm or chilled, you'll be glad to be in the Promised Land with a glass of this in your hand.

Makes 2 cups

2 cups organic 2 percent milk

2 teaspoons Savannah Bee Company Tupelo honey, or your favorite honey

1 teaspoon vanilla extract

Sprinkle of cinnamon or cinnamon sticks

Heat the milk, honey, and vanilla. Pour into mugs if serving warm, or chill and serve in a glass. Sprinkle with cinnamon, or allow the cinnamon to infuse by garnishing the warm milk with cinnamon sticks.

Strawberry Blonde

What a perfect name for a lovely drink! Taking the fiery redness of strawberries and blending it with the calming color of cream will result in the most beautiful pink drink to serve your friends and family. When strawberry season is at its peak, this drink is fabulously delicious. Serve with a dollop of whipped cream and you have strawberries and cream in a drink!

They say gentlemen prefer blondes . . . well, this gentlemen will take a Strawberry Blonde any day!

Serves 4–6

2 cups strawberries, tops removed

1 cup 2 percent milk

1 ¹/₂ cups heavy whipping cream

¹/₄ cup powdered sugar

1 teaspoon good vanilla

Ice, optional

Whipped Vanilla Bean Crème
Fraîche (see page 85)

Blend strawberries, milk, cream, sugar, and vanilla together until fluffy and smooth. Add ice to the blender for slush, if desired. Garnish each glass with a dollop of Whipped Vanilla Bean Crème Fraîche.

Water Infusions

✸ Cucumber Water ✸

Agua frescas are mainstays in Latino culture. This "water refreshment" takes a cue from the garden. For the freshest of refreshing summer delights, cucumber ice water is de rigueur. Cucumbers, with their mild flavor and cooling aura (think "cool as a cucumber"), make for lovely discs of summer goodness to float in a pitcher, jar, or bowl of water.

Garnished with mint, basil, limes or additional cucumbers, this easygoing, placid drink should surely cool down the hottest of summer days.

Makes about 1 gallon

1 gallon water

4 cups ice

1 medium cucumber, sliced into rounds

Make ice water in a large pitcher. Float the cucumbers in the ice water and allow their essence to infuse the water for at least 10 minutes. The longer the cucumbers are immersed and stay in the water, the stronger the flavor. Kept chilled, this will stay fresh for a couple of days.

❋ Herbal Ice Cubes and Sparkling Water ❧

It is often the simplest of gestures in life that make for elegant entertaining. With amazing refrigerators and ice machines galore in our homes, the old-fashioned method of freezing water in ice trays has almost gone by the wayside. I keep some of those ice trays around to make herbal ice cubes. My friends and family are always glad to have a treat in their ice, and the presentation is memorable and aesthetically pleasing.

The crisp shapes and forms of the lovely aromatic leaves bound in ice is the perfect accouterment for sparkling mineral water. Whenever I travel outside the country, I love being asked by the servers if I'd like water "with gas" or "no gas"; this drink reminds me of those travels.

As the ice melts in the sparkling water, the herb leaves release their essence so the scents, bouquets, and flavors meld with the fizz, creating beverages of pure delight and refreshment. Flavor with a syrup or citrus, but trust me: this severely clean-tasting drink is fine on its own.

Fill an ice cube tray with a leaf or two of your favorite herbs, such as rosemary, thyme, basil, and mint, and then cover with water. Place in the freezer until frozen and use for sparkling water or any drink, for that matter.

Waking-Up Water

Water is life's liquid. Served sparkling, flat, tepid, warm, cool, chilled, bottled, or on tap, this is the universal drink of choice. Yet, with just a simple twist (say, of a lemon or lime) this simple beverage can be woken up and served with zesty zeal and pizzazz. Here is one of my favorite recipes for water and a splash of juice—refreshing anytime.

Makes 2 servings and a tad more for seconds

5 cups crushed ice

1 cup cold water

**3 tablespoons freshly
squeezed lemon juice***

*Try lime, nectarine, Meyer lemon, orange, or any fruit juice of your choice. Waking-Up Water is easy and fun!

Place all ingredients in a blender and cover. Blend for 10–15 seconds.

❋ Ahhhh—Agua Fresca ❋

Refreshing water, or "fresh cold water"—just the name of this classic drink in English or Spanish is delightful. One is basically taking plain water and adding some fruit for a medley of refreshment. Easily made for a crowd or just a couple of folks, this beverage lends itself to interpretation and also the season.

Often made with melons, pineapple, or tropical fruit, agua fresca can be served in a myriad of ways. Ladle up glass after glass of this refreshment for your own porch or party!

Serves 8

10 heaping cups of your fruits of choice*

1 cup Simple Syrup of your choice,
   Basic or Herbal (see page 5 or 6)

1/2 cup freshly squeezed lemon juice

1/2 cup freshly squeezed lime juice

8 cups water

One 10-pound bag ice

Fruit for garnish—the same
   kinds as you pureed

*Cantaloupe, watermelon, and honeydew make gorgeous colored agua fresca. I like to mix pineapple and strawberries for a luscious colored batch of this too!

In a food processor or blender, puree your fruit of choice. Be sure to scrape down the sides to get all the goodness! Add the simple syrup and lemon and lime juices then puree again until smooth.

Into some glasses or other large serving vessels, pour in the fruit puree and then add water and ice to the desired consistency. Mix well and ladle up!

✳ *Index* ✳

apple cider, in Indian Summer
 Apple-Ginger Sparkler, 47, **47**
Apple Cider, Spicy, 58, **59**
apple juice:
 Birthday Party Punch, 78
 Pear-Apple Slush, 57
 Spicy Apple Cider, 58, **59**
apple, in Pear-Apple Slush, 57
Apricot nectar, in Apricot Velvet, 34, **34**
apricot nectar, in Mango Lassi,
 Y'all (*see* footnote), 38, **39**
Arnold Palmer, An, 14

blackberries:
 Blackberry Fizz, **48**, 49
 Blue Lagoon, 63
 Deep Dish Blackberry Tart, 50
 Mayflower, **72**, 73
 Sweet Tea Southern Sangria,
  24, 25
blueberries:
 Blue Boy/Blue Belle, 64, **64**
 Blue Lagoon, 63
 Blueberry Oatmeal Drink, 62
 Brown Sugar Blueberry
  Pound Cake, 65, **65**

cantaloupe, in Agua Fresca
 (*see* footnote), 94
cherries:
 Mama Temple, 31
 Sweet Tea Southern Sangria, 24, 25
Chocolate Cake, Basic, 28
coconut, in Ambrosia Nectar
 with Coconut Rim, 32, **33**
coffee, in Café au Lait Du Pre, 26, 27
cran-grape juice, in Birthday
 Party Punch, 78
cranberries, in Berried Treasure, 60, 61
cranberry juice:
 Berried Treasure, **60**, 61
 Georgia Sunrise, 70, **70**
 Mayflower, **72**, 73
Cucumber Water, 91
cucumber, in Mobile Mary
 Tomato Nectar, 35, **35**

Farmer's Tea, 10, **10**; *also:*
 A James Farmer, 14, **15**
 Raspberry Mint Tea, **18**, 19
 Sweet Tea Southern Sangria, 24, 25

ginger ale:
 Birthday Party Punch, 78
 Blackberry Fizz, **48**, 49
 Indian Summer Apple-
  Ginger Sparkler, 47, **47**
 Peach Julep (*see* note), **52**, 53
 Sparkling Grapefruit Drink, 51, **51**
grape juice, in Birthday Party Punch, 78
grapefruit juice, in Sparkling
 Grapefruit Drink, 51, **51**
grapefruit, in Ambrosia Nectar with
 Coconut Rim (*see* note), 32, **33**
grapefruit, in Sparkling
 Grapefruit Drink, 51, **51**
grapes, in Birthday Party Punch, 78

herbs:
 basil:
  Herbal Ice Cubes, 92, **92**
  Herbal Simple Syrup, 7
  Honeydew Green Tea, **12**, 13
  Mobile Mary Tomato Nectar, 35, **35**
  Summer Herb Peach Tea, 11, **11**
 lavender:
  Herbal Simple Syrup, 6
  Lavender Limeade, **36**, 37
  Summer Herb Peach Tea, **11**
  Sweet Tea Southern Sangria, 24, 25
 lemon thyme:
  Herbal Simple Syrup, 6
  Summer Herb Peach Tea, 11, **11**
 mint:
  Farmer's Garden Mint Shake, 84
  Honeydew Green Tea, **12**, 13
  Mint Simple Syrup, 6
  Orange Spooner, 42, **43**
  Peach Julep, **52**, 53
  Raspberry Mint Tea, **18**, 19
  Summer Herb Peach Tea, 11, **11**
  Sweet Tea Sorbet, 22
  Sweet Tea Southern Sangria, **24**, 25
  Watermelon Sweet Tea, 23
 rosemary:
  Blackberry Fizz, **48**, 49
  Farmer's Garden Wassail, 68, **69**
  Herbal Simple Syrup, 6
  Honeydew Green Tea, **12**, 13
  Mobile Mary Tomato Nectar, 35, **35**
  Mrs. Wilson's Rosemary
   Lemonade, 44, **45**
  Rosemary and Pecan Crème
   de la Crème, 81

Summer Herb Peach Tea, 11, **11**
 Sweet Tea Southern Sangria, **24**, 25
Honeydew Green Tea, **12**, 13
honeydew, in Agua Fresca
 (*see* footnote), 94
Honeysuckle Cordial, 74

ice cream:
 Farmer's Garden Mint Shake, 84
 vanilla, in Apricot Velvet, 34, **34**
 vanilla, in Rosemary and Pecan
  Crème de la Crème, 81
iced tea (Farmer's Tea), 10, **10**

Julep, Peach, **52**, 53

lemon juice:
 Agua Fresca (*see* footnote), 94
 Blackberry Fizz, **48**, 49
 Ginger Pink Lemonade, 41, **41**
 Mrs. Wilson's Rosemary
  Lemonade, 44, **45**
 Spicy Apple Cider, 58, **59**
 Waking-Up Water, 93
Lemonade:
 Ginger Pink, 41, **41**
 in An Arnold Palmer, 14
 Mary Ann, or Traditional, 40, **40**
 Mrs. Wilson's Rosemary, 44, **45**
lemon(s):
 Honeysuckle Cordial, 74
 Mama Temple, 31
 Mary Ann, or Traditional
  Lemonade, 40, **40**
 Sweet Tea Sorbet, 22
 Sweet Tea Southern Sangria, **24**, 25
lime juice:
 Agua Fresca (*see* footnote), 94
 Blackberry Fizz, **48**, 49
lime(s):
 Lavender Limeade, **36**, 37
 Mama Temple, 31
 Pomegranate Cooler, 75, **75**
 Sweet Tea Southern Sangria, **24**, 25
 Watermelon Punch, **76**, 77

Mango Lassi, Y'all, **38**, 39
milk:
 Blue Boy/Blue Belle, 64, **64**
 Café au Lait Du Pre, 26, 27
 Coconut Cream and
  Pineapple Puree, 82, **83**

95

Index